With It
—or—
in It

Desert Shield and Desert Storm from the Loader's Hatch

Bacil Donovan Warren

Acknowledgements

In the process of creating this memoir there are many people to whom I owe enormous debts of gratitude.

Foremost, my parents CW4 (Ret.) Bacil C. (RIP) and Gail Warren, and my brother Ed. They all unconditionally supported my decision to enlist, and have been my inspiration all my life.

Philip Kwong, my tank Platoon Leader and friend who reviewed and gave invaluable feedback on this work. He also brought back every solider he took to the sandbox alive with no wounded—with it, not in it. Brave Rifles, Sir!

Robert Bell, my barracks roommate, best friend, and one-time Driver (on C-66), who also gave invaluable feedback on this work.

Jamie Davis (@podmedic), author, Paramedic, nurse, friend and writing mentor. His initial feedback on this work led to substantial improvements, and I can't thank him enough for his patience.

Richard Roscoe—friend, Paramedic, and former co-worker who gave feedback on an early version of this story.

I would also like to acknowledge my NaNoWriMo writing buddies on the Internet: Sam Bradley (@SamBradley11), K. M. Vanderbilt (@KmVanderbilt), and B. A. Wilson (@BAWilsonWrites). My interactions with them have improved my writing and my life in measurable ways.

And, finally, to AF and TK, my interactions with whom have inspired me to self-examine and become a better man. Without their inspiration, I would still be languishing inside my own mind, trapped in the past.

Contents

Chapter One:
The Path to the Shield

Part 1

August First, Nineteen Ninety. Approximately Seventeen-Thirty hours local time, Mountain Daylight, on the back line of a Tank gunnery range in Doña Ana, New Mexico.

At the time, I was a SPC (Specialist, enlisted rank E-4), technically assigned as the Gunner on C-66–the tank of the Troop commander–in C ("Cyclone") Troop of the US Army's 1st Squadron, 3d ACR (Armored Cavalry Regiment): the "Brave Rifles." We had just returned to Ft. Bliss, Texas, from an extended TDY ("Temporary DutY") deployment to Ft. Hunter-Ligget in central California. Now, much of my Troop, as well as A ("Apache") and B ("Bandit") Troops and D ("Dragon") Company, were split up to cross-fill–that is, to temporarily fill in on another unit's tank, to bring their crew up to a full four members for a training exercise–for 2nd and 3d Squadron units preparing to deploy to the NTC (National Training Center) at Ft. Irwin, California.

In the approximately fourteen months that I'd been assigned to C-1/3ACR, I think we'd spent about ten and a half of it in the field. With all our field training, I hardly knew my barracks room (though, I knew how to get back to it from Juarez after a night of drinking). I definitely didn't know the girl I'd been seeing very well, as it turns out she'd been sleeping with several other soldiers from the base, something I only found out after getting back from TDY. And in a plot twist I'd only ever seen in pulp fiction, I was assigned to cross-fill as a Loader on a tank where the Gunner was one of the soldiers with whom she'd been cheating on me.

I knew Doña Ana range pretty well, though, and I knew that if you tuned the Auxiliary radio ("Aux") over to the extreme low end of the frequency range, you could pickup the local TV channel 13 audio transmission, and it was time for the national news. We were waiting for sunset, which in this part of the desert sometimes doesn't come until about 20:00 hours (8 PM), and the chow truck had just pulled up, so I knew we'd have a few minutes to relax.

Doña Ana Range, NM, part of Ft. Bliss. This would be your view if you were looking off the left side of the turret from the Loader's hatch of an M1A1 tank. And it happened to be sometime in 1990.

As I fine-tuned the Aux and pulled in the transmission, the Gunner stuck his head into my loader's hatch.

"Warren, pull that speaker out will ya?"

There's an attachment for a field phone to the radio system in the M1A1 tank, and it can be wired for all kinds of sound output devices, including headphones, speakers, and others. I pulled out the field speaker and wired it up, then passed it up so he could set it on the top of the turret so that the whole crew could listen to the news.

That night's lead story might not have engendered much discussion, most of the time: one nation in the Middle East had a dispute with another, and their dispute led to conflict. That kind of stuff happened all the time, it seemed. It was about Iraq invading Kuwait: a small, C-shaped, oil-rich Arab nation, situated on the eastern side of the Arabian Peninsula between Iraq and Saudi Arabia. At the time, I could have told you where it was, and really not much else. Iraq seemed to think that Kuwait was illegally drilling into their sovereign territory, and overproducing their quota of oil, and felt the only way to solve the problem was to invade and take over.

Really, what the story was about was that all of our lives had just taken a turn for the surreal—with apologies to CPT Miller, from Saving Private Ryan. Something was different. We all felt it immediately, as evidenced by the stunned silence from the rest of the soldiers gathered around our turret. I immediately knew what it meant, and thought to myself "we are going to end up over there because of this idiotic invasion." I didn't mean to say it out loud, but I did and got an immediate nod of agreement from the Platoon Sergeant.

Not five minutes later, it was our tank's turn to rotate over to the chow truck. Unsurprisingly, it was T-Rations. The T-Ration is a field ration the Army frequently feeds to soldiers in the field and consists of large sealed trays (hence, "T") of food heated by immersion in hot water. I don't remember the main meal but I am pretty sure the starch side was scalloped potatoes. We geared up and waddled over, grabbed chow, and sauntered back to the tank. In the field, M1 tank crews often consume their meals on the front slope of the tank, and tonight's was no different ... except that no one was chatting. There was no BS-ing, no complaining about the quality of the food, no good-natured ribbing one another about the ugliness of the other's sister or whether or not she was good in bed. In fact, there was a lot of silence. A lot of sounds of eating, some shuffling of feet on rocky dirt, and the speaker on the turret, nattering on about the baseball scores with nobody much paying attention.

That's how you knew when you had a tanker's attention. Not when they were rapt to your words, not when they were in formation following you with their eyes, as these are things all soldiers are trained to do. It is when they are standing around, milling about, but nobody was saying anything. It was right at about the end of evening nautical twilight when there is just a ribbon of silver light on the horizon and dark, dark blue to black above it when the loudspeaker on top of the Range Control Tower sparked to life:

Guidons, guidons, guidons. Be advised that at approximately Sixteen Hundred hours Mountain Daylight Time tonight, the nation of Iraq invaded Kuwait in an unprovoked act of aggression. All units are ordered to stand down from training and await further orders, out.

"Guidons" was radio-speak for "All units on this frequency" and when repeated like that, also substituted for the phrase "BREAK" which means all units be silent and listen for important traffic.

With that, we refocused on offloading the ammunition in the tanks and then did a road march back to the motor pool. We spent the night in the barracks at the range. First thing in the morning we assisted with getting the tanks ready to head back to Ft. Bliss. Then we mounted the trucks the Regiment sent for those of us who were cross-filled to begin the trip back to Ft. Bliss and our original units.

From the Driver's hatch of an M1A1 tank, looking up at C-92 on one of the tank gunnery ranges. Doña Ana, NM, part of Ft. Bliss.

Part 2

Coming back to Ft. Bliss after having been "unassigned" from our cross-fill duties, we weren't absolutely sure what was next. We did feel reasonably confident that we were being re-tasked for a deployment to the Middle East. As a result, the next few weeks proceeded as an orgy of changes. For most of the three or four decades prior to Iraq's invasion of Kuwait the 3d ACR along with all of III Corps had been preparing, training, and planning for–and stood ready to execute–a REFORGER mission (REturn of FORces to GERmany) with a specific focus of reinforcing the US Army Europe in the event of a Warsaw Pact invasion of central Europe. That alone required the Brave Rifles to completely shift gears, since it was not the grassy plains of Northern Germany nor the thickly forested Bavarian and Hessian hills and mountain ranges and valleys of the Fulda Gap, but the vast emptiness of the Arabian desert that would see the first combat deployment for the Regiment since WW II. Not that we were unfamiliar with desert warfare. We were stationed at Ft. Bliss, TX, in El Paso and did all of our local training either in the desert surrounding the base or in Doña Ana, NM, only a few miles away. We also did rotations to the National Training Center at Ft. Irwin, CA which is an even more unforgiving desert than that found near El Paso, and is actually pretty similar to some parts of the Arabian Peninsula in its geography: lots of sand and rocks, long stretches of flatness interrupted with stretches of rocks and sand.

Shoulder patch for the 3d ACR

I should give some background here. The 3d ACR was a bit of an outlier in the US Army, only one of three units of its type on active duty. The other two were the 2nd ACR and the 11th ACR, both of which were stationed in Germany at the time. All of the ACRs owed a long train of history to old horse cavalry—as do all armored units in the US Army, really—but were a kind of a hybrid organization. Historically, cavalry units are reconnaissance and shock troops. This has been true going back through the days of horse-mounted rifle units (the Light Brigade of Tennyson's poem, for example), mounted knights with lances and heavy armor, to the light skirmisher & scouting units of the Celts of Central Europe and the Huns of the steppes, Carthaginian war Elephants and Numidian cavalry, Macedonian Companion Cavalry, and the light horsemen of Persian armies just to name several. In the more modern era, since the introduction of the "tank," cavalry in the US Army has served two primary roles: reconnaissance (also called scouting) and speedy application of combat power. Many WWII cavalry units were assigned with light tanks (the M5 "Stuart" and M24 "Chaffee" for example), which sacrificed heavy armor and high-caliber, high-power main guns for speed and maneuverability, or used scout cars such as the M8 "Greyhound" to perform their duties. In the role of scouting, stealth and speed are imperative: the cavalryman must arrive at the place he means to observe without himself being observed, and must be able to get there and back out again as quickly as possible. This remains true even yet and was definitely true in 1990. However, there were these three oddball units in the ACRs. The ACR was a Corps-level asset; meaning, it was the recon unit for an entire US Army Corps, an organization with multiple Infantry or Armored Divisions and commanded by an LTG (Lieutenant General, a 3-star General). The Corps is a massive organization; during the Cold War, the 11th ACR was the Corps ACR for the US Army V (Fifth) Corps in central Germany, and V Corps defended the Fulda Gap—an approximately 130 kilometer-wide, 110 kilometer-deep parcel of land stretching from Fulda to Frankfurt am Main—with two divisions in Germany (the 8th Infantry and the 3rd Armored) and approximately 65,000 soldiers.

While scouting was also the role of even smaller cavalry units, such as the DIVCAV (Divisional Cavalry) squadron of the 3rd Armored Division, the ACR had a fairly unique place, and organization, in the Army. The ACR was a Regiment, rather than a Brigade—the term for a similarly sized unit in Infantry or Armor units, commanded by a Colonel (O-6)—owing to its more direct lineage from the horse cavalry units, which used that term. It was larger, in terms of both personnel and equipment, than the Brigade-level equivalent in infantry or armor organizations. The ACR had more artillery, and it was assigned lower in the chain than was true in similar, non-ACR units. The ACR had a similar sub-organization style to an infantry or armored Brigade and was composed of 3 cavalry Squadrons (called a Battalion in most other units, and commanded by a Lieutenant Colonel, O-5), each consisting of 3 cavalry Troops, a tank Company, and a howitzer Battery. There was also an Air Cavalry Squadron, and one Support Squadron. Each Cavalry Troop commander in an ACR had two 120 mm mortars as part of his Troop, something unheard of in infantry or armor companies (Troop, in the cavalry, is the same level as Company in infantry or armor, or Battery in artillery, commanded by a Captain, O-3). Each Cavalry Squadron had three cavalry Troops with 12 M3 "Bradley" CFVs (Cavalry Fighting Vehicle) and 9 M1A1 "Abrams" tanks and was the scouting part of the Squadron. The Squadron also had a heavy Company, which was a standard tank Company of 14 tanks, and an integral howitzer Battery. Organizationally, this gives a cavalry Squadron of an ACR 41 M1A1 tanks (a standard tank Battalion would have 58, and a standard infantry Battalion none) and 41 M3 CFVs (none in a standard tank Battalion, and 58 similar M2 Infantry Fighting Vehicles in a standard infantry Battalion), with 8 M109 self-propelled howitzers. In terms of size, it's about 80% of a tank Battalion plus about 80% of an infantry Battalion, with organic artillery all the way down to the Troop level (not the tank company, though). Pound-for-pound, the ACR was heavier and more flexible than an equivalent armored or infantry Brigade.

Why all the differences? That is a mission issue: the ACR, its Squadrons, and its cavalry Troops, must scout for the Corps commander and deny enemy forces the ability to do their own scouting. A standard tank Battalion will defend, or will attack, and may perform other missions, but the cavalry Squadron will also do:

- area reconnaissance (scout a specific place, often an important terrain feature or built-up area);
- zone reconnaissance (scout all things within a defined zone);
- route reconnaissance (scout a particular road or route of movement or communication through an area); and,
- screen lines (basically, establish stationary or moving observation and firing locations, to give the Corps commander early warning of enemy attacks or defensive locations),

as well as other reconnaissance missions that the tank or infantry Battalion simply cannot, because they don't have the equipment or the personnel. ACRs also do hasty and deliberate defense, as well as hasty and deliberate attack missions, just like infantry and tank units. In so doing, they need firepower in addition to mobility and stealth. The ACR and its subordinate Squadrons & Troops are often the first units to locate enemy forces, and may be forced to act before the Corps commander has time to process what has happened—sometimes before he is even *aware* of what has happened. It is, therefore, task-organized to be much more self-reliant than the infantry or tank Brigade or Battalion.

Thinking back, I don't recall exactly what day the official orders were announced—I believe it was sometime in mid-August—that the 3d ACR was no longer an asset for the III Corps, but had been reassigned to the XVIII Airborne Corps. At the time, the XVIII Airborne Corps consisted of the 82nd and 101st Airborne Divisions, and the 24th Infantry Division. We were ordered to begin preparations to deploy to the Kingdom of Saudi Arabia as the cavalry Regiment for XVIII Airborne Corps. From that point for the next few days, we spent almost all of our workdays on finalizing the physical equipment for transport to the theater, culminating in a final railhead along with US Army Reserve units who specialize in logistics. My tank, *Cool Breeze*, was on a flat car on her way to Beaumont, TX, to be loaded onto a US Navy RORO (Roll-On, Roll-Off) ship for the long float toward the Persian Gulf.

One of the changes that occurred was a change in my assignment. While I had been the Gunner on the Troop Commander's tank, C-66 (a.k.a "Black 6" in the shorthand radio parlance), almost the whole time I'd been at Ft. Bliss, along with the orders for the re-assignment came a change of personnel including an influx of NCOs (Non-Commissioned Officer). With no TC (Tank Commander) spots open in the troop, one of the NCOs was reassigned to be the Gunner on C-66, and I was moved to the Loader's spot on C-21. C-21, the aforementioned *Cool Breeze*, is the tank of 2nd platoon's Platoon Leader. A Platoon Leader is normally a 2nd Lieutenant (a commissioned officer, rank O-1) or 1st Lieutenant (O-2). I was not at all happy about it; being a Gunner in an M1A1 tank is one of the best jobs in the Army—bar none. However, I understood the reality of an NCO doing an NCO's job, and a Specialist doing a Specialist's job. Due to my experience as the Gunner on 66, which often resulted in me being a de facto Tank Commander, the Platoon Leader of 2nd platoon gained a tremendously experienced self-starter for a Loader, a real asset for a first-time Platoon Leader. This was in addition to already having as his Gunner an NCO with a long history of experience, including stints as a TC in the past.

Two soldiers from 3d ACR performing tank maintenance just before taking the tank to the railhead.

With our tanks (and Bradleys, and all of our crew-served equipment along with most of our other medium & heavy equipment) en route to the Gulf, we spent a lot of time doing classroom training, a change for a unit that had spent more than 70% of the last 14 months doing field training. Our classes included Vehicle ID, platoon & troop sandbox training, as well as UCOFT gunnery. The UCOFT (Unit Conduct Of Fire Trainer) was a computer-based tank gunnery simulator, highly customizable and very good for training Tank Commanders and their Gunners in the crew actions of fire commands, conduct of fire, and action drills. It doesn't involve the entire crew, however, so those of us who were neither Gunners nor TCs were often tasked with detail work: painting, cleaning, and so forth, when we were not doing other training exercises.

Another of the changes required us to do a considerable amount of learning about the Iraqi army, their armored systems, their tactics, their small arms & crew-served weapons, and the experience of the Iraqi army during the 8–year long Iran/Iraq war. The last part was the one most frequently drilled into our heads: the Iraqi army, and especially the Republican Guard, was a battle-hardened army with years of combat experience in the desert. We were constantly warned not to underestimate their ability to wage war. We were reminded that there had been reports of chemical attacks by the Iraqis, and to expect that any actual conflict with Iraq would result in chemical attacks. We were constantly tested on this point. "GAS GAS GAS" screams from the senior NCO staff or the tripping of an M9 chemical alarm on purpose happened frequently enough to be annoying, but the reminder was always the same: you will die, with mustard gas in your lungs or with nerve agent on your skin, if you don't take the threat seriously.

We also did some non-standard training, for a Regimental Armored Cavalry Troop with just under half of its personnel being tank crewmen. We practiced Close Quarter Battle (CQB) and urban warfare as dismounted soldiers. I'd been stationed in Germany before coming to Bliss, and in neither place was it ever really a consideration for tankers to dismount and take the fight to the enemy on foot. At least, not unless there was a temporary situation involving a tank that was completely inoperable, but where the tankers needed to continue fighting anyway. Now we did, practicing storming the barracks with one-half of the troop acting as defending OPFOR (OPposing FORce, the "enemy force") and the other as the attacking BLUEFOR (BLUE FORce, or "friendly forces"). It was fun, exhausting, and enlightening for tankers who hadn't really done much of that in the past.

There was also one completely unexpected side benefit: nearly every day, we were "released" (that is, no longer expected to be "at work" and "on duty") at the after-lunch formation. So, usually somewhere around 13:00 to 14:00 we would have our formation, receive any updates, and then be dismissed for the day. I don't recall ever being told specifically why, but it always seemed to me that it was a command decision to allow the Regiment, especially those with families, to spend as much time with their families as they reasonably could before we deployed to the Gulf. To those of us in the barracks, however, it was just extra party time—and boy, howdy, did we take advantage. I will spare the lurid details, but I will just mention that the proprietors of Spanky's, Cosmos, the Cave (as we called it, not necessarily the actual name of the establishment), Tequila Mockingbirds, and a whole host of other establishments in Ciudad Juàrez, Chihuahua, Mexico, were probably quite happy between August and October of 1990. Yes, soldiers sometimes drink when they are off-duty.

As August stretched into September, training continued and some of our troop mates were discharged as normal. There was a stop-loss order for soldiers whose ETS (Expiration of Term of Service) dates were after a certain date, but there were a few whose ETS dates were before that and they were allowed to separate as they normally would.

In the last few days of September, we received the official order to deploy. An Advanced Party was set up and flew out to the Kingdom of Saudi Arabia. An Advanced Party consists of a few Officers, NCOs, and enlisted soldiers who leave ahead of the majority of the rest of the unit, called the "main body," and coordinate the main body's arrival. The rest of us stayed behind, cleaned the barracks to within an inch of its life, and stored all of the personal items we would not be able to take with us to Saudi in our wall lockers. Then, on 30 SEP 1990, we locked them, witnessed them being banded and secured, drew our service weapons and tank sidearms (for tankers in the 3d ACR, that would be the M9 Beretta semi-automatic pistol for each crew member, with two M16A2 rifles per tank), and loaded our personal gear and ourselves onto a 747 to begin our long flight. This particular aircraft was a Hawaiian Airlines 747, mobilized by the DoD (Department of Defense) as part of the CRAF (Civil Reserve Air Fleet). With military airlift capabilities stretched to their limit at that time, the CRAF provided needed airlift options for the DoD, and we were lucky enough to get a great aircraft with a great crew.

We flew to Kansas City for a short stop, then onto Nova Scotia (in neither place, deplaning), and then to Frankfurt. Once at Frankfurt, we did deplane, with about a two-hour layover in the USO facility there on base. We were able to make brief phone calls home, play ping-pong and foosball or watch TV, and stretch our legs. We also took advantage of a time-honored US Army tradition of leaving our mark; the USO had arranged to have butcher paper placed over a couple of the walls of the recreation area and had pencils and pens available with which we could graffiti on them. Soon we resumed our flight, and took off for Greece. A short layover in Athens, then a hop to Saudi Arabia, and we disembarked into a night of still-brutal heat and dryness.

Even though I was from the desert of Arizona, and had been living and training in a desert for the 16 months prior to arriving in Saudi Arabia, the very air of that desert seemed to suck the moisture out of my skin. It is how I imagine the Fremen felt without stillsuits, on the desert planet Arrakis, from Frank Herbert's science fiction novel *Dune*. Upon deplaning for this final time, we were urgently handed a single liter bottle of water and instructed to immediately drink it. We were further ordered to drink water at every opportunity, to fill our 2 two-liter Desert Canteens whenever we had the chance, and to maintain our awareness of our exertion level to avoid becoming heat casualties. Our Path to the Shield ended here; we were officially the Desert Shield.

Chapter Two:
Desert Shield

An Aspis Aloft

After chugging our water and claiming our personal bags & equipment from the belly of the 747 contracted to deliver us unto the Sandbox we mounted transport trucks (most of them the 2.5-ton truck known affectionately as the Deuce & a Half). We moved into a warehouse. We were in the port of Jubail, issued a cot and told where to set up to sleep. Our platoon sergeant, a little whip of a man with a drawl and a penchant for fast cars, set up a platoon plan for the storage of personal gear, and initiated a sleep plan for the platoon as soon as we hit the floor of the building. Tank crews set up cots in a group, with the entire platoon in one area near to each other. We stored our personal gear as per our Platoon Sergeant's plan, and set about implementing the sleep rotation.

We spent just three days in the port. On the second day, the RO-RO (Roll-On Roll-Off) ship with our equipment on it docked nearby. We offloaded our equipment into a makeshift motor pool. First order of business was to check over the tanks, to make sure that all the parts & tools were present and functional, and then start them up to make sure they were in running order.

As a tanker, I can tell you there is little as soothing, as awe-inspiring, as nearly orgiastic as the dulcet sounds of an entire squadron of M1A1 tanks turning over their turbine engines. The whine and whistle of the final phase of startup, a rising crescendo of whistle and screech, culminating in a throaty whoosh of rushing exhaust, is as orgasmic a sound as exists, to a tank crewman. To hear all 41 of the Squadron's tanks start up in quick succession was the first real sign of the awesome power our military would flex in the weeks and months to come. Next, we ran all the self-tests and did our Preventative Maintenance Checks and Services (PMCS) and made sure to store as many of our things as we could on the tank. We were working so hard, we hardly noticed how hot it was: 110° F+ on the concrete pad, despite being only a few meters from the Persian Gulf waters. I didn't notice until I felt something weird and sticky on my chest. It was my tee-shirt. At that time, we were mostly in our "chocolate chip" desert BDUs (Battle Dress Uniform). While working on the tanks we were usually permitted to remove our BDU top and work in our tee-shirts. It was plastered to my chest, and white crusty edges had formed in any place where my sweat had evaporated. I looked at the temperature gauge for the ammo compartment: 130° F. No wonder I was sweating so profusely: it was hotter than Hades. That brought back the warning of a couple of days before to drink water every chance we got. Now, it was clear why, because it was easy to lose track of how hard we're working, and how fast we're losing water!

Lunch time came, we ate, and continued to work. Despite the temperature concerns, the Regiment issued a nearly complete service load of ammo for all our weapon systems. This included the 120 mm Main Gun, all three machine guns, as well as personal weapons and sidearms. As a result, armed guards began to patrol the motor pool area.

We spent one more night in the warehouse. The next day, we proceeded to load up the tanks with most of our personal equipment and gear, save our rucksacks & sidearms. At just about noon we started to load our tanks onto Heavy Equipment Transport (HET) trucks, one tank per truck, for a road march to our offload point in the middle of nowhere. We traversed the TAP Line Road, a road which was used for access to the Trans-Arabian Pipeline, northwest for several hours. Sometime about 21:00 (9 PM) or so we stopped, off-loaded all of the HETs, and assembled our vehicles. When we reported ready, our Troop Commander led us out into the featureless (and extremely dark) desert. We drove in a column formation for several more hours, and finally arrived at our designated Assembly Area. After setting perimeter security, we implemented a guard & sleep plan, and were able to bed down for the few remaining hours until sun-up.

To this day, the first night I spent in Saudi Arabia out in the deep desert is still one of my most cherished memories. Disregarding for a moment the reason for my presence— and the danger that would unfold there—it was as peaceful and serene a night as I've ever experienced, before or since. With the tanks all shut down (at least their engines), and no other vehicles operating, the only noise was the occasional shuffling of feet or clanking of metal objects, as someone closed a vehicle hatch or dropped a tool. Wartime night operations call for strict light discipline, and tank crews such as you find in the 3d ACR are quite adept at it. Because of that, not only were there no city lights but also no local ones to interfere with my vision of the bejeweled heavens above: a veritable blanket of black with our own, personal, thousand points of light gleaming down. I recall being on the front deck of my tank, with my Driver and one of my other buddies, just admiring the stark contrast: utter, universal beauty above, and sheer horror around, until we finally gave in and settled into sleep.

C-22 off in the distance during Exercise Imminent Thunder, somewhere in the middle of the Saudi desert

We didn't get much sleep; the arrival at the AA (Assembly Area) was approximately 02:30 and sunrise in the desert there was around 05:30 or so. The squadron command staff gathered, selected a location for our Base Camp, and we executed a short movement to what would become Base Camp Bessey (named after one of the Regiment's earliest Medal of Honor winners, in 1877), and our home for the next couple of months.

Once in Base Camp Bessey, we resumed a normal routine: exercise in the very early morning, breakfast, tank maintenance or training, lunch, more tank maintenance or training, inspections, dinner, and nighttime personal hygiene. Speaking of ... Showers, and body cleansing. At first, it was the so-called "whore's bath": soap, water in an empty ammo can, and a washcloth. Rub mostly in the stinky parts of the body, followed by a rinse. Then, the engineers constructed a reasonable facsimile of a shower facility. There were three of them; two 4-person stands for men and a single 2-person for women. I don't recall there being any women in the Squadron; there might have been a couple in the HQ element, but I don't think so. There were MPs and attached logistic and supply units, which may have necessitated the separate facilities. In any event, the facilities were great, but the water was usually quite cold. When it got really pretty darned cold, like at night, the water in the showers would get just as cold so everybody took a cold shower. On the plus side, knowing the shower water would be cold meant nobody lingered: everybody got exactly as wet as needed, soaped & shampooed up, then got exactly as rinsed as needed, and nobody took too long. Eventually, the engineers who built the showers figured out a way to get an immersion heater in the water supply, and that meant we could take warm showers.

At first, the tents we received for the base camp were donations from local Bedouin tribes and were just big enough for a single tank crew. After about a month or so in Base Camp Bessey, Squadron issued larger tents. I seem to recall it was both 1st (Scout) platoon, and 2nd (Tank) platoon who lived in our new, larger tent.

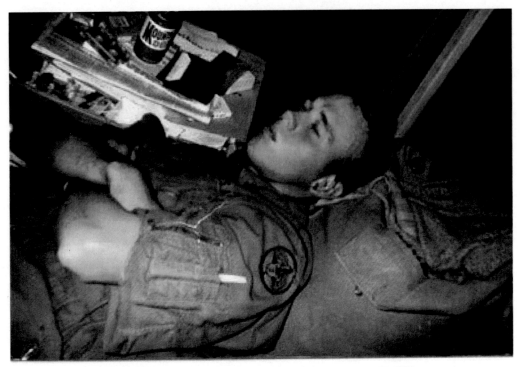

The author, ambushed by a camera while sleeping in the luxurious new GP Medium tents

After the first few days, when it became evident that we were not going to be immediately attacked by the Iraqis, base camp activities took on a more businesslike air. There was always the threat, however, that we'd be surprised by the Iraqis, and we maintained our tanks every single day regardless. Of course, our tanks still had live, service ammo (as opposed to training ammo) loaded in them, and we did in-camp training all the time. Tanks require pretty constant maintenance to run smoothly, but sometimes even well-loved tanks such as *Cool Breeze* have gremlins that make maintenance a challenge. *Cool Breeze* and all the rest of the Squadron's tanks were some of the first M1A1 tanks issued anywhere in the Army, and had many hundreds of engine hours on them by the time we were deployed to Saudi Arabia. Our particular gremlin liked to make the engine abort for no apparent reason. The maintenance guys all the way up to Regiment knew our tank, and had been investigating these engine problems for years, but were never able to uncover any cause for it, nor fix it. It didn't happen often enough to be able to pin down, but when it did happen it was always a huge pain. So for the next couple of months, we spent quite a lot of time trying to isolate this gremlin.

Some of our training in camp consisted of old reliable tanker training tools like the sandbox exercise, so named because often there was an elevated table with sand in it which could be shaped to resemble terrain features like hills and slopes and so forth. For desert soldiers, though, the sand on the ground worked very well. We did lots of vehicle ID training, and continued covering the Iraqi ground and air force tactics. One troubling thing in particular was the Iraqi artillery, which was reported to be quite numerous. Most tanks, and the M1A1 tank in particular, offer exceptional protection from artillery fire and shrapnel. Enemy artillery is less of a threat to the tanks and their crews than to the scouts—particularly dismounted scouts—and the combat support vehicles like trucks, HMMWVs, and lightly armored tracks such as those operated by the medics and maintenance personnel. But even for tankers, artillery is a threat for other reasons. It can force tank crews to button up—close all their hatches and stay cooped up inside the tank—which reduces visibility and the crew's situational awareness, making the crew a little bit less effective. It can deliver (or, threaten to deliver) chemical weapons, forcing crews to don the Mission Oriented Protective Posture (MOPP) gear including the protective mask, which degrades the crew's fighting ability.

In addition to our small-unit training, we also did specific training exercises as a Squadron, and Regiment. During November, we were part of Exercise Imminent Thunder and practiced several action drills as well as squadron and troop roles in the offense and defense: movement to contact, deliberate attack, hasty attack, hasty defense with counter-attack, zone & area reconnaissance, and so forth. In particular, during part of this exercise, one of our higher headquarters started a simulated chemical weapons attack, and "GAS GAS GAS" screams came out over the radio. We immediately donned our masks and MOPP gear, and fought some of our "battles" during Imminent Thunder at full MOPP level 4 (all protective equipment on). It was hot, miserable, sweaty, stinky, and extremely annoying.

The author at MOPP 4 during Imminent Thunder

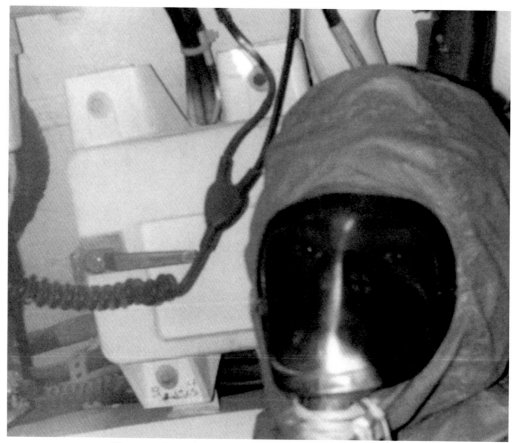

My gunner, SGT Planter, also at MOPP 4 during Imminent Thunder

It wasn't all training. Soldiers, like anyone, need some kind of down time occasionally to maintain their sanity. We had sports events; volleyball and flag football were both favorites. Somehow, one of the members of Cyclone Troop was able to get a fairly complete set of weights delivered to them, including a bench. That allowed soldiers who were interested in doing more than just the normal PT to also lift weights. There was also often time after the day's activities were completed when we could just hang out in the tents and read, listen to music, or enjoy Armed Forces Radio. Mostly, AFN broadcast music, sanitized news, and sporting events (I was able to hear my Arizona Wildcats play at least one football game).

That would be SSG Miller, 2nd (Tank) Platoon, C-1/3 ACR, setting a dig. Naturally, 2nd Platoon dominated.

We also read and wrote letters. While this is always a treasured activity for soldiers, during Desert Shield it was even more special than usual, partly owing to the astonishing number of "Dear Any Soldier" letters we received. Whenever this mail would arrive, we would eagerly pick a few letters each and devour them, then respond to their authors. Most of these letters were sent by school children, which meant that we felt even more proud to write back and justify their investment in our well-being. Some were sent by fellow young adults, college students or just people in the public, and a few were from vets from prior conflicts.

And as much fun as it was to receive and reply to these correspondences, the real joy came from the mail we received from friends and family. Just after we deployed to Saudi Arabia, my maternal grandfather passed away. He had been present at Pearl Harbor, training as a B-17 navigator and bombardier when it was attacked on 07 DEC 1941, and so it became even more important to me to keep in touch with my grandmother and parents to make sure they knew I was still okay. My paternal grandfather was a big Arizona fan as well (most of my family attended the U of A), and sent clippings from the sports pages of the Arizona Daily Star to keep me updated on the football team's exploits. Friends from El Paso and Las Cruces would send letters and pictures, as well as cassette tapes. It was always a great escape, to be able to lie back in bed with a flashlight or "chem light" and read about our family or friends and their activities. The "chem lights" (as we called them) were the safety lightsticks made by Cyalume, which were heavily used by the US Army. Every tank had a couple of cases of these chem lights in several different colors, and they were much preferred to most other artificial illumination.

There were other activities that occurred while we were in Base Camp Bessey, probably the least fun of which was the burning of the poop. Yes, you read that correctly! Our latrine facilities were a wooden stand with holes cut out for us to sit over, where we could do our business. The lower portion of most of the latrine was wood but the upper part was a fine mesh screen which kept the insects pretty much out but also meant that there was virtually no privacy for using the facilities. Under each spot for using the facilities was the bottom portion of a cut-out 55 gallon metal drum, to which was affixed handles and in which was deposited a slurry of some kind. The slurry helped to keep the smell down, but included a small amount of flammable material I believe to be diesel fuel. At least once a day, a detail was formed to pull these out of the latrines and set them on fire, so as to destroy the waste. This, please believe me, is nothing you will ever want to smell in your life if you can avoid it. It was easily the worst detail we did in base camp.

Once Imminent Thunder completed and we returned to Base Camp Bessie, our regiment received a warning that we had new equipment coming. Each tank platoon in the regiment was tasked to send a small detail to head out to King Abdulaziz port in Dammam to help offload them when they arrived. I was assigned to this detail, and spent Christmas and New Year's both in port waiting for the ship with our new equipment to arrive. After about two weeks of sitting at the port literally bored to tears, our ship arrived. In a frenetic twelve hours of work we offloaded the Regiment's equipment from the ship, and delivered it to the DOD civilians who were responsible for initial testing and final painting (desert sand this time instead of green). Although there was a lot of nothing going on most of the time we were on this detail, there were a couple of things that I recall. First was that besides our presence in the warehouse, other units started to arrive. The Coalition decided to increase the troop presence in Saudi Arabia, to give them an offensive military option if necessary. As a result, after being in the port for several days we got some company. The US Army's 1st Infantry Division (the "Big Red One") started filling the warehouse and offloading their own equipment, including tanks, Bradleys, HMMWVs, and so forth. Because these units were starting to flow into the port, AAFES (the Army and Air Force Exchange System, the people who run some of the retail stores on Army and Air Force bases worldwide) opened a nearby branch PX (Post eXchange). The PX (the Air Force calls them "BX" for Base eXchange) sells various sundry items like cassette tapes, batteries, soap, toothpaste, books, and other such items. If you will think of it kind of like Target®, but run by the AAFES. Being in Saudi Arabia, they didn't sell some items they would normally carry, like alcoholic beverages, but they did carry some of the things we soldiers miss the most when in the field or otherwise forward-deployed. At one point during this detail, I was able to buy a copy of INXS's new album X, featuring the singles "Suicide Blonde" and "Disappear," both of which made it into heavy rotation on my Walkman® Sport alongside my normal repertoire of Judas Priest, Metallica, AC/DC, Anthrax, Megadeth, and Iron Maiden.

While our detail was basically waiting for the influx of these new arrivals to clear the port, I had the opportunity to run into a couple of old friends. Once, while in the line for this PX, I ran into my very first Platoon Leader and TC when I was stationed in Germany: 1LT Sauer. He was a West Point grad and upon my arrival with C Company, 3/8 CAV of the 3rd Armored Division I became his gunner. We spent a lot of time in the UCOFT training and got pretty good as a TC/Gunner team. He was one of my favorite leaders, and while we were only able to chat for a few minutes it was nice to have a chance to meet up with him. I also ran across a couple of old tanker buddies from 3/8 CAV, and we also chatted for a bit.

As nice as it was to reunite with my old buddies, it was also an ominous reminder: we were all here, all in the same place, to rain death and destruction upon an enemy—should our nation ask us to do so—and possibly have it also rain down upon us. I recall the sinking feeling in the pit of my stomach as that realization came up, that this might be the last time

I talk with any of my former tank mates. A sobering realization, that.

The night we were shipped back to our units from the warehouse in Dammam was one I'd blocked out of my mind for a long time—so much so, that in the first version of this book, I inadvertently left it out. When we were finally released from our detail—all of our new tanks and Bradley vehicles were off-loaded from the *Lash Atlantico*—we collected all of our gear, and boarded a bus to return to 1st Squadron, where we'd eventually get transit to our respective Troops. The bus, an old, old Blue Bird yellow school bus that would not have garnered a second look in the rural United States in the 1960s, would take us down the TAP Line Road toward our unit's newer position. During our stay in Dammam, 3rd ACR had struck their base camps and taken up residence in a more forward-deployed position. Although I was not given any official reason why (and never asked, either) I assume it was because of the influx of new units that resulted from the political decision to present a ground offensive capability. That included the earlier-mentioned 1st Infantry and 3rd Armored Divisions, as well as several other units who were assigned to the US Army's VII Corps from Germany. Where our base camp was originally located south of the border with Iraq, now the Brave Rifles were in a field posture, preparing to zero and fire gunnery on their new tanks and Bradleys somewhere south along the Wadi Al-Batin. This was quite a bit further west than we'd originally been positioned.

The night that we boarded the bus to return to our units was a miserably cold, rainy night. Stiff winds were blowing from the northeast and bringing with them freezing cold rain, at times limiting visibility to only a few hundred feet. We traveled along the TAP Line for a couple of hours and then stopped while the convoy commander came and talked to the bus driver. After a short, heated discussion I couldn't hear, the commander left and the bus followed his vehicle into the desert.

Yeah, I couldn't believe it either. A Blue Bird yellow school bus, trying to keep up with an HMMWV across the desert landscape of Northeastern Saudi Arabia, in a blinding, freezing rainstorm. After about thirty or forty minutes of being badly jostled around the bus, we stopped. The convoy commander had also stopped and then he came back, and I could see why the bus driver stopped: there was a massive puddle in their path, and even the HMMWV driver didn't want to chance driving through it. Eventually, we were ordered to put on our Kevlar helmets and brace ourselves, as the bus was going to have to attempt to get through this obstacle. There was no other way.

I was sure I was going to die that night.

We all complied, and braced ourselves for what may come next. The HMMWV driver gunned his engine and plowed through the puddle. It was passable but deep. Our bus driver did the same thing: engine revved, thrown into gear and ZOOM off we went. We hit the edge of the puddle, which slowed our momentum and everybody pitched forward in their seats. "Not like this" was the only thought I could muster. "Not like this." The engine revolted a bit, but kept running, and we kept moving forward. Although we were tossed around a bit none of us got hurt and the bus finally made it through to the far side.

I'd love to say that was the end of that night's misery, but apparently it was only getting started. Once we finally arrived at the link-up point, there was an HMMWV waiting there to take those of us from 1st Squadron back to the Squadron TOC (Tactical Operations

Center). There, we would stay overnight and in the morning Cyclone Troop would send a vehicle to retrieve their troopers (as would each other Troop and Company in the Squadron). It was still raining. Not a deluge, but a constant, driving, bitter cold wet spit from an even colder, driving wind.

Since we were spending the night at the Squadron TOC, once we arrived we set about trying to find a place to sleep. Since the TOC is mostly made up of supply, maintenance, and command vehicles—not the combat vehicles we usually attended—finding an unoccupied flat(-ish) place to lie down for sleep proved to be nearly impossible.

"Why not sleep on the ground?" you might ask. Well, there are a couple of major reasons not to do that. First, in most mechanized and motorized units, at least in the US Army, there is usually an SOP (Standard Operating Procedure) against sleeping on the bare earth except in quite specific circumstances. The reason for the SOP prohibition is founded in the other major reason: it's extremely dangerous. The operators of nearby vehicles may not be aware of your presence on the ground, and may run you over; even if they are aware, they may forget where you are and thereby kill or seriously injure you. Sleeping on the ground, therefore, was right out. Finally, after about an hour of schlepping around the TOC looking for a safe, dry-ish and warm-ish place to lie down, a couple of us came across one of the maintenance deuce-and-a-half trucks. It was the only place left we could find, so we informed the driver (who was sleeping in the cab) that we were back there and made do.

We climbed in the back, and tried desperately to find any place to lie flat. What we got was a truck with a bed full of steel and aluminum parts: Bradley and tank road wheels, road wheel arms, sprockets, hatch covers, and other assorted parts. Being metal, they were all freezing cold. We tried lying on them anyway. After about another hour of fighting our bodies and the cold metal, we discovered the worst part: the canvas roof of the truck was not watertight, and was dripping and leaking ice-cold rainwater. We tried to find the least dripping part of the bed, and finally got so tired we didn't care anymore how wet, cold, and miserable we were. It was about 0300 (3 AM) when we finally fell asleep. Two hours later, we were roused by the driver, and informed that our ride was here.

That was the best news I'd heard in many days.

So after having spent about three-and-a-half months in Base Camp Bessey, the Brave Rifles had moved out to a new AA. We were back to living and sleeping in and on our tanks, something with which we had quite a lot of experience. While in our new AA, as I was about to take responsibility for a guard shift, I heard the news over the radio: war had begun.

Chapter Three:
Desert Storm

The Storm Starts

On the back deck of an M1A1HA (HA for Heavy Armor) tank somewhere in the middle of the Saudi Arabian desert north of TAP Line road and to the south of Kuwait I sat. I was a nervous but confident 21-year-old Specialist, sharing the latest happenings on the BBC news broadcast in my earphones with my Troop-mates huddled nearby. My 9 mm M9 Beretta, loaded but not locked, was secured in my shoulder holster; my M16A2 rifle (also loaded, but not locked) sat cradled in my arms. Just a few hours before, my Commander in Chief George Herbert Walker Bush, the 41st President of the United States of America, had broadcast on radios and televisions worldwide that the allied Coalition had let Saddam Hussein play out the full measure of his rope, and was about to start hanging his military forces with it. I listened to some of the news reports, relaying to my buddies the information that BBC rebroadcast from CNN. Peter Arnett was at that moment making CNN famous worldwide by reporting on Coalition air strikes in real-time from his hotel room in Baghdad.

The author, left, and his Gunner debate the merits of M1A1 pack replacement vs. repair. Base Camp Bessey, Saudi Arabia, sometime in Oct–Nov 1990

The beginning to Desert Storm was, by all local accounts, a non-event. Nothing had really changed for the Brave Rifles, as we'd been expecting an Iraqi invasion of Saudi Arabia since early October. As a result, our guard was already up, and long so. It did bring a certain inevitability, I think, to hear the reports about the air strikes, and wonder somewhat apprehensively how the Iraqi army would react to these initial attacks: would they hunker down and wait it out? Would they come up swinging and launching chemical or even nuclear weapons as they did so?

So it was that I then took the earphones off, handed the Walkman Sport off to one of my nearby platoon mates, securely fastened my Kevlar helmet and strode off to assume the beginning of my two-hour guard shift. I recall as I was patrolling between tanks—spaced some 50-100 meters apart—being hyper-aware of the environment around me: sandy rocks, mostly, with infrequent undulations in the terrain perfect for hiding an Iraqi commando and a stockpile of grenades. There weren't any Iraqi commandos there, at least none that started throwing grenades or otherwise made their presence known, but I started recognizing then how much more vigilant I must be if I wanted to get back to the States and take my Troop-mates with me. It did certainly coalesce then, knowing that it was now a virtual certainty that the only way back home was through Iraq, and through the Iraqi Army in the process.

My guard patrol shift ended without incident, and after I awakened my relief (my best friend and barracks roommate, Specialist Bell), I located and retrieved my Walkman. After Bell roused, geared up, and took over his shift, I eased down into the loader's hatch of my tank and replaced my Kevlar with my CVC helmet—a thinner helmet for Combat Vehicle Crewmen, with an integrated padded liner and headphone/microphone—and then pulled out the book with our radio frequency assignments and double-checked that all of tomorrow's frequencies were properly programmed on the radios. I then connected my Walkman to the intercom system of *Can't Touch 'Dis*, the glorious 70-ton piece of war machine I had called home for the past couple of weeks. Our old steed, the M1A1 *Cool Breeze*, had been replaced (as had all of the tanks of the Brave Rifles regiment) at the end of December with the updated M1A1HA, one of the pieces of equipment my detail had retrieved from the port of Dammam in late December & early January. The HA variant included additional armor especially on the turret and hull front, which was known to contain depleted uranium (although the exact composition was, and remains, secret). *Cool Breeze* was a bit of a hag, long in the tooth (having been used with the 3d ACR since 1987) and filled with electronic gremlins, but had served us remarkably well despite her tendency to abort the engine for no reason whatsoever. Her replacement, in *Can't Touch 'Dis*, was an immaculate, flawless gem of a machine, however, and we didn't miss the older jezebel even a little.

While updating the radios, and familiarizing myself with the soon-to-occur challenge-and-response change (it was nearly midnight, local), I heard the familiar tones of BBC's breaking news. In the space of the next thirty seconds, things went from serious, but manageable, to near-petrifying, as BBC outlets in various towns on the western border of Israel were reporting air raid sirens, gas-mask messages, and explosions: Iraq had decided to try to turn the war with the US-led coalition into a Jihad against the Jews, and was launching scud missiles at Israel in an effort to force an Israeli counter-strike. Such a move might seriously jeopardize the coalition, at least where our Arab allies were concerned, and it was widely understood (even if vehemently denied) that the Israelis would likely counter chemical warfare with nukes.

And at that moment, I was maybe more terrified than I have ever been, at any moment before or since. Later, during the ground war, I was forced to fire my Loader's M240 machine gun at an enemy soldier to prevent harm to myself or my tank crew, but even the later realization of what happened wasn't as bone chilling as that radio broadcast.

Fortunately, as we all know now, the US promised to Israel that we would make Scud targeting one of our highest priorities, and we sent them several batteries of the Patriot missile system, and the Iraqis never did put chemical weapons in those Scuds (or, at least, I believe they did not), and so the Israelis did not intervene. But for the next few hours, the mood in our little corner of the world was somber, indeed.

The View from Here

After several days of the "air war" (as I believe it was called by the news media), the Brave Rifles received a new mission and new orders. We were to pack up, HET our vehicles westward up the TAP Line Road, and occupy a screen line to observe for any possible enemy attempts to penetrate the Saudi border from the west of the old neutral zone between Saudi Arabia and Iraq. Dutifully, we did so and assumed positions along a line just a few kilometers south of the actual border. Scout platoons were dug into positions where they could overwatch a large valley, with the tank platoons in a more central, hide location with OPs (Observation Posts) just downslope of the ridgeline, occupied 24/7 in a rotation from tank to tank. Loaders and Drivers were the primary occupiers of the OP, with the Gunner of the tank currently on rotation stationed in the designated tank on the TC's .50 caliber MG. Any activity in the valley was immediately called up to the on-duty tank Gunner over a field phone, who then clarified the information and if needed relayed the information with a standard report format up to the troop command net, who did the same up to Squadron. Not much happened, though; the desert out in that part of Saudi Arabia and Iraq is trackless, mostly featureless, and nearly impossible to navigate safely without advanced equipment (like, say, GPS). There were occasional sightings, mostly of Bedouin tribes shepherding their livestock (often goats) through the area, but rarely anything of military value.

An example of the flat, featureless terrain of North-Central Saudi Arabia & South-Central Iraq

One night in particular was pretty tense, however. Since the air war had been going on for a few days, it was not unusual to hear (and, rarely, see) aircraft making runs overhead. They occasionally flew with their various lights illuminated until they were almost overhead of us, and then extinguished them as they penetrated northward into Iraqi airspace. On this night, however, one of our sister units to our left or right flank very excitedly reported aircraft circling nearby, and since neither Squadron nor Regiment could identify these aircraft we all leaped into action. At first, it was difficult to find them; the directions we were getting from higher headquarters were confused and conflicting, but eventually our Gunner, SGT Planter, was able to locate the circling aircraft using the thermal sights. On the thermals, jets can be hard to track even in the widest view due to their speed, but he was able to get it done. After several minutes of watching and waiting, with updated information about their location, SGT Planter identified the aircraft: two F-15s circling a KC-135 fueling aircraft—friendlies. The LT immediately sent up the report to the troop commander, who consequently ordered all units to hold fire (not that we would do much good anyway, at the ranges involved) and repeated the information to Squadron. While I feel reasonably sure the tank crews would not have had much impact from a fratricide perspective—the effective range of the tank main gun is about three or so thousand meters, and these aircraft were almost certainly six to eight thousand meters up—there were ADA (Air Defense Artillery) assets with us as well. I can't prove it, but I think SGT Planter may have saved several AF pilot and crew member lives that day.

At one point during our deployment on this screen line, we also had an opportunity to meet with the boss man himself: General "Stormin'" Norman Schwarzkopf, the CINC (Commander IN Chief) of 3rd Army and US Central Command, as well as the overall commander of all Coalition forces in the theater. He came around each of the various commands in 3rd Army, and we had a chance to hear him speak and ask questions. We listened to him discussing the progress of the air war to date, share with us information about what kind of forces we were facing, and his overall vision for how we would execute a ground war if it became necessary.

Yes, that's correct: we were still hoping against hope for a peaceful solution. Combat arms soldiers do brutal things and have brutal things done to them if war breaks out. Even though we trained for years for exactly this event—not knowing it would ever actually happen, of course—it would still be preferable for us to be part of a rattling saber, rather than a drawn one if possible. Combat soldiers know how awful war is, which is why we'd rather not engage in it.

So, he explained everything to us, gave us a few moments to ask questions and pose for pictures, and would be on his way.

At the time, we'd been on the screen line for a couple of weeks without any mail delivery. When the time came, there were a few questions that came up. As is my way, I waited to see if anyone else would ask the question I had in my mind, but when nobody else asked I raised my hand. General Schwarzkopf recognized me to speak.

"Sir, Specialist Warren, Cyclone Troop. We've been out here for two weeks without any mail. When can we expect it?"

He looked thoughtful for a moment, then leaned over to his aide, and whispered in his ear. The aide left, and he replied "soon, I promise."

Later that evening, two weeks' worth of mail arrived in the Cyclone Troop TOC (and, I presume, the rest of 1st Squadron). I can't say for sure that I had anything to do with that, but I'd like to think so.

The OP duty was usually a few hours at a time, two soldiers in the foxhole with a camo net, fire plan, binoculars, night vision goggles, and both a PRC-77 radio (emergency use only) and a field telephone wired up to the guard tank—one tank, C-22 as I recall, on-station in a turret defilade position that permitted the NCO of the guard to bring the Thermal & Daylight sights of the tank onto anything reported by the OP, as well as use the .50 cal as an immediate action weapon. I never minded the OP (some did), although I'd still rather be on the tank than off.

There were other occasional activities that came up; mail, once it started arriving, was always a welcome one. As I'd mentioned earlier, not too long before Iraq's invasion of Kuwait I had the misfortune of being cheated on by my girlfriend (with whom I broke up, on learning this news). Afterward, I had met a few other young women at New Mexico State University in nearby Las Cruces, NM, several of whom maintained contact with me and a few of my troop mates via postal mail. We received letters, and care packages, and occasionally audio tapes, which was very cool. I wish I still had the tapes! One of these friends was very clever in writing to me; Saudi Arabia forbade items like "nudie" magazines (Playboy, Penthouse, etc.), so those rarely (if ever) were received by the soldiers, but they didn't often (if ever) seem to worry about individual letters to the soldier. She wrote her letters on the torn-out pages of magazine ads, featuring very seductively posed and clad models (never nude, though!). That kind of morale-booster was always welcome, especially by a 21-year-old man stuck in the desert with a bunch of other (mostly) 20-ish-year-old men!

Most of these letters were about the various goings-on in their lives, reassuring us that we were still remembered, and admonitions to come home safely—to paraphrase the Spartan women, to come home "with it" ("it" being our tank) rather than "in it." If we came home in our tank, would mean that we'd been killed in action, leaving part of ourselves inside a tank destroyed by the enemy.

One other incident sticks out in my memory from this time. We had been on this screen line for at least a couple of weeks, as I recall, and it may even have been close to the middle of February (and, thereby, close to the start of the ground campaign, Operation Desert Sabre). It was nearing dusk, and we'd been hearing a bit of an uptick in air activity overhead for a couple of days. I recall hearing what I thought might be an aircraft well overhead, but it was tough to tell, and then we saw the tell-tale signs of an over-the-horizon Iraqi unit using air defense: tracers into the air, and some mid-air explosions. As we tensed up and geared up in case we needed to rapidly remount our tanks, I saw what for all the world looked like a freaking laser beam, from the sky to the ground: Bright red-orange, in a straight line down to the ground just over the horizon, two or three times. As I stood there completely enchanted by the sight, trying to process what happened, I heard the sound: BRRRRRRRRRRRRRRP. BRRRRRRRRRRRRRRRRRRP. BRRRRRRRRRRRRRRP. An AC-130! The AC-130 is a weapons platform version of the C-130 cargo plane, carrying (among others) a 105 mm cannon and a pair of 20 mm Vulcan 6-barrel Gatling guns. A couple of my platoon mates standing nearby started to whoop & holler, and I joined in with them. Tankers appreciate heavy weaponry, regardless of its source, and the AC-130 ranks third behind the second-place A-10 Warthog as a tanker's favorite weapon platform (their own tank being #1).

After several weeks of being in the deep desert, watching our screen line, we were temporarily relieved by another unit (whose identity escapes me). We withdrew back toward the Squadron combat trains and Tactical Operations Center (TOC), where we were rotated onto Deuce-and-a-half trucks and told to bring our personal hygiene kits and a change of uniform. We drove out into the desert a bit and were delivered to a US Air Force air base of some kind or another, only a few kilometers south of our position, where they had a fully-functioning hot shower for thirty people set up. We took a glorious shower, under tents and with a seemingly unending supply of hot water, shaved, got all together tidied up in a way we hadn't been able to get in many weeks, then changed into clean duds (well, clean Combat Vehicle Crewman (CVC) suits, the fire-retardant Nomex suits worn by tankers in battle), and went back to the Squadron TOC for a hot meal as well. T-Rations were the order of the day for us on the screen line for most meals, and today's meal was still T-Rations, but this time we got to eat them sitting at an actual table and actually hot, not just still-warm from the mermites (portable food transport containers) on the front deck of the tank. There was also a Class VI supply truck there. Class VI refers to items of a more personal nature such as hygiene supplies, beverages, snack food, and batteries. I was able to stock up on batteries, cigarettes, and some pogey bait (snacks, candy, chips, and so on). We re-mounted the tanks, relieved the unit sent to relieve us and resumed our screen mission.

Finally, on the evening of the 23rd of February, we struck our site and road marched to a new AA. Although we'd been getting mission briefings and OPORDs (OPeration ORDers) continuously through our deployment, tonight's became the final OPORD for the ground campaign. We did our PMCS, and ate dinner while the leaders did their prep and meeting with the troop CO, then got our final OPORD: at noon the following day, local time, the Brave Rifles would launch an attack across the Line of Departure and begin moving toward a series of objectives, with the ultimate goal of destroying any enemy forces we encountered, reaching a particular objective a dozen or so kilometers south of the Euphrates, and then turning East to cut off the Republican Guard from escaping back into central Iraq. The LT finished briefing the platoon, and we executed our guard and sleep plan and bedded down for the night. We slept solidly, knowing that the next day our Sabre would be unsheathed.

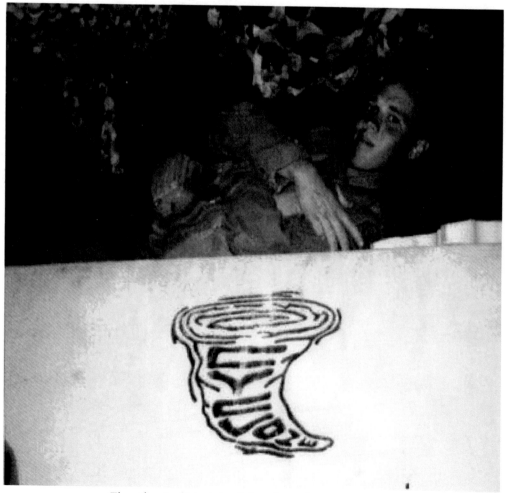

The author atop his tank, just before going to sleep on 23 FEB 1991.

Chapter Four:
Desert Sabre (Ground War)

A Sabre, Drawn

It's about 14:30 local time (2:30 PM), 24 FEB 1991. Charlie Two-One—a.k.a. *Can't Touch 'Dis*—approaches the berm at a moderate speed. Our engineers have cut a couple of fine holes in the "impenetrable tank barrier" that Saddam's forces erected to keep us out of Iraq, just not very wide ones. In fact, they're not much bigger than an M1A1HA tank is wide, and therefore, we must exercise some prudence in our speed. Just a few minutes before the TC on our wing tank C-22, SSG Miller, had led the 1st (Scout) and 2nd (Tank) platoon in an impromptu prayer, asking for protection as well as the guidance and wisdom to do right and come home safely, and then the ammo and fuel trucks came by for a final top off. The M1A1HA tank, like the M1A1s we'd turned in, carries 40 rounds of main gun ammunition in the various storage racks.

Our storage racks were already filled with ammunition, but there was one place left to fill: the actual gun breech. I loaded the HEAT round—High Explosive Anti-Tank, a round intended to defeat older tanks and light armored vehicles with a shaped charge warhead—into the main gun breech, and then assisted SGT Planter in topping off our fuel before we received our final order to cross the Line of Departure—the berm just ahead of us, marking the borderline.

Our tanks carried two types of main gun ammunition, HEAT and Sabot rounds. The Sabot round was the primary round we would use against the top-line enemy tanks, such at the T-72. Since our intelligence had predicted all of the T-72s were with the Republican

Guard, we didn't "battle carry" the Sabot round. We instead loaded the HEAT round because we expected to see mostly lightly armored infantry vehicles and old tanks, such as the T-55, which our HEAT rounds could easily penetrate.

Approaching the breach in the berm

The "impenetrable tank barrier" being penetrated — and, rather easily, I might add

The crew of *Can't Touch 'Dis* is a motley one. Our TC is a 2nd Lieutenant, LT Kwong, and recent graduate from the University of San Francisco's ROTC department. In addition to being our TC, he is also the Platoon Leader of 2nd (Tank) Platoon of Cyclone Troop. The tank's Gunner is a SGT (Sergeant, E-5), SGT Planter, an excellent Gunner and tanker who had occasionally gotten himself into trouble; he had been a SSG (Staff Sergeant, E-6) at one point in his military career. Our Driver Errol Thomas, another Specialist like me, is an outstanding one. He was a bit of a wiseacre and came into the Army by way of the hoods of Detroit—or, maybe, Compton, California. Our TC listens to Adult Contemporary, classical, and a smattering of country and AOR/Top-40 music. Our Gunner enjoys country, rock, and rap/hip-hop, while our Driver listens almost exclusively to hip-hop.

The author, left, and SPC Thomas, right—posed shot and not actually fighting (not here, anyway)

I, of course, am the Loader. Mostly, I listen to heavy metal & hard rock, and I control the radio/intercom system. That is part of my job; the Loader, in addition to loading the 120 mm main gun as well as the 7.62 mm coaxial machine gun and operating the loader's M240 7.62 mm machine gun, is responsible to the TC for operating & maintaining the intercom and radio systems on the tank. Even though we don't all agree on the musical choices, I am obligated to make sure we all get our music played through the jury-rigged system in the intercom, even if I don't particularly like some of it.

Just as the tank's intercom system can be wired to output sound to an external speaker, there are also methods for connecting input to the intercom. The method I learned was to sacrifice a pair of crappy headphones, strip the wires, and connect the stripped sections to the input posts. I was, fortunately, smart enough to realize before we deployed that a well-protected Walkman would come in tremendously handy, and bought a Sport Walkman with AM/FM radio and Auto-Reverse, and always made sure to get as many AA-batteries as the supply sergeant could locate or buy myself when the Class VI truck would come to the assembly area.

Since we'd known for a while there was a 100% certainty we were going to be performing a ground attack, and to within a few dozen hours when it would occur, there was the final important piece of the puzzle to consider. What song do you play over the tank's internal intercom as you ride a 70 ton beast of depleted uranium, steel, and rubber into the largest ground offensive in decades?

There's the old standby of "Die Walküre", by Wagner, made famous by the movie *Apocalypse Now* as the music choice of helo flyboys—or, maybe just insane Air Cav regimental commanders—everywhere: too cliché we decided. After some reasoned debate (a rarity for our crew), I quoted the lyrics to a Metallica song from the 1987 album ... *And Justice for All*: "The Shortest Straw". We all agreed that it fit perfectly our vision for the fate of Saddam's military. They'd made us come 10,000 miles, live in a forsaken, dreary hell-hole of a desert for six months, and we were damned if they were going to stand in the way of our getting back home.

As we sallied through the breach, nerves afire and eyes ablaze with the focus of battle-to-come, we heard the epic and prophetic refrain from the song. The shortest straw had been pulled for them, and it was time to deliver the news.

A Borderline, Crossed

After the initial fear and Zen-like focus of crossing into Iraq, the rest of the day of the 24th (24 FEB 1991) generally progressed in a distinctly un-terrifying way: we ran into essentially no resistance, and met all of our objectives without incident. Due to our initial good fortune we were traveling at a good clip, which meant we had to refuel fairly frequently. Refueling in the field is dicey enough, but add the stress of being in an active combat zone (even if we weren't actually being shot at right that moment), and it became downright frightening. Of all the things I did as a tanker, the first refueling operation inside Iraq during the ground war was one of the scariest. Imagine this: you're standing on the back deck of a tank, with a fire extinguisher and an open fueling port, watching to see that the fuel tanks don't become overfilled. First, you're standing on top of the tank. As opposed to, say, being safely ensconced inside the 70 ton (combat loaded, less kits) beast made of rolled homogeneous steel, a secret blend of other armors, and depleted uranium, as any sane person would be. Second, you're in a situation already known to be dangerous enough that US Army protocols dictate a soldier stand right there with one of the tank's portable fire extinguishers in his hands while you're performing it. Third, at any moment, an enemy unit, helicopter (*shudder* perish the thought), or aircraft might get lucky, and catch you with your pants around your ankles refueling, which makes you a fantastic target for being shot. And, as if that weren't enough, fourth (and finally) my eyes, and the eyes of my tank's Gunner, SGT Planter, were on the fuel level, not the horizon, meaning our particular tank would be caught wholly unprepared if an enemy were to appear. We were not alone, there was air cover, the 4th Squadron (Long Knife) of the 3d ACR had Kiowa and Apache helicopters nearby, and the rest of our own Squadron and Troop were setting security while refueling operations were in progress. That knowledge does not alleviate the anxiety, just for the record. We would wind up refueling a few more times over the ground war, none of which were quite as tense as the first one.

Looking back toward the Combat Trains — the collection of maintenance, medical, supply, and other non-combat vehicles — of C Troop, 1/3 ACR

As we continued on, day drifted into night as a blanket of dark dropped over the featureless and empty desert. Navigating in this terrain is next to impossible during the day, but at night it becomes truly impossible ... unless you have GPS, which was brand-new then. So brand new, in fact, that we had exactly 2 GPS receivers in the Troop, one with the CO in C-66—the Troop command tank—and one with the XO (Executive Officer, 2nd in command of the unit) with the combat trains. They would communicate occasionally over the Troop's logistical radio frequency to ensure they stayed on course (and to avoid communicating over the combat/command net, which was kept mostly radio "quiet" for combat communications only). As the tank's Loader, it is my responsibility to keep air guard, when I'm not actively loading the main gun or performing other duties inside the turret, so I kept my focus—and machine gun—pointed toward the rear-left of the tank. I didn't see much of the desert in front of us, but I got good looks at the things we passed. With the onset of evening, I retrieved the night vision goggles and kept them around my neck for easy access if necessary. The Troop stopped just long enough for the vehicle's drivers to insert their own night-vision equipment, and then we resumed our march. That first night brought the first problem: during our march, we came across some elevated road surfaces that bypassed an unseen feature of the terrain (and, to this day, I still have no idea what it was). The Driver of our scout platoon leader's Bradley misjudged the edge of the roadway, and it rolled over the edge of the embankment injuring the platoon leader and one of the other scouts in the vehicle. We continued on, with the 1st (Scout) Platoon Leader jumping onto another Bradley to stay with his soldiers despite his injury.

Destroyed enemy vehicles as we pass them, northbound

Dawn the second day (25 FEB) came, and we started to run into pockets of enemy resistance. Occasional firefights would break out, and since C Troop was (along with B Troop) the front edge of the Regiment's right flank, we caught a lot of these as we swept north toward the Euphrates River Valley. Mostly, what would happen is that one or other scout platoon would observe enemy defensive positions, the tank platoons would come up and exchange a volley or two of fire with them, and they'd surrender. Sometimes, the enemy troops would surrender when the Bradleys came into view. We began routing hundreds and hundreds of POWs back through the MPs and continued our advance. The closer we got to the Tigris and Euphrates rivers, the more frequently we would encounter enemy resistance. This continued unabated for all of the second day, night, and third day (26 FEB).

Starting on the night of the 26th, things became much more ... interesting, let's say ... and after two days and nights of unbroken advance across a trackless, formless desert, we paused: for an attack on a small town, occupied by a built-up tank and mechanized force of 2nd-tier Iraqi troops (that is, not the Republican Guard—we were still quite a ways from them—but the topmost tier of the regular Iraqi army). We got a radioed FRAGO (FRAGmentary Order, a partial order for new combat operations), then halted in place and set security while the Regimental HQ initiated an artillery and rocket barrage on the town's defenders. After about an hour and a half of an artillery barrage, we executed a hasty attack on the edge of the town. Several firefights broke out, and a few Iraqi tanks were destroyed, but after a few minutes, these soldiers surrendered just like all the others had.

During all of our operations, we continued to have basic, normal human needs: eating, drinking, using the latrine. We had a vast stock of MREs (Meal, Ready to Eat) on each tank, so food was never an issue. We also had a vast stock of water, believe it or not; each tank went into combat with (as I recall) four cases of 1L bottles of water, plus each of us had two full 2 Liter desert-issue canteens inside the tank, and drank from them frequently (the bottled water, mostly, went into refilling the 2 Liter canteens when they became empty). Many of us—including me, myself—also had a crippling addiction to caffeine, and since we weren't stopping hardly at all, it became more and more difficult to make coffee when blood levels became too low for sustained wakefulness. I had caffeine pills (Vivarin® was a favorite), but I preferred to save them for the utmost end of need. Instead, I took to essentially eating the instant coffee packets from the MREs. Only two of us on my tank, SGT Planter and myself, really drank coffee anyway, so it was easy to score the packets from both SPC Thomas and the LT. I'd take two of them and a sugar packet, rip them all open together and dump their contents into my mouth. One swig of water later, and it was done. It's not the tastiest way to ingest caffeine, but the mother of invention being what she was, it was my only real option. We continued rolling along, picking up POWs (Prisoner Of War) along the way, and making great time to our objectives.

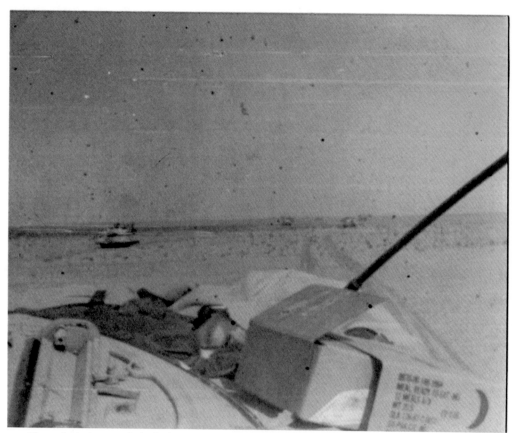

The author's view over the back of C-21's turret, looking back at C-22 and the rest of 2nd Platoon, C Troop, 3d Armored Cavalry Regiment

Final Delivery

The night of the 26th gave way to the morning of the 27th, and we had made our big right turn and headed straight into the northern edge of the Iraqi positions. Just a bit to the south of us, 1st Armored Division was fighting a major engagement with the Medina Luminous division (Medina Ridge), while we were plowing through a couple of Iraqi divisions and—along with the 24th Infantry Division, to our north—closing the Iraqi escape routes to the river valley.

Sometime after about 1400 local time on the 27th, we had moved into blocking positions and received orders to halt and consolidate our positions and forces. Our platoon sergeant, SFC Young, set a sleep plan, and I was fortunate enough to be selected to be the first on our tank to get to sleep. I grabbed my Nomex jacket as a pillow, jumped out on the back deck of the tank, and it took about two seconds to fall into a deep slumber ...

... so deep, that the next thing I knew I was being jostled awake rudely by SGT Planter who was kicking me as hard as he could on the bottoms of my boots, screaming "GET UP GET UP GET UP" as loud as he could muster at me. At first, I didn't understand what was going on. "Why is he screaming at and kicking me?" I thought to myself, as I slowly realized that he wasn't the loudest thing going on at that moment. He was screaming because the sound of the Iraqi artillery falling all around our position hadn't woken me up, and it was the most noise he could make at me without actually hitting me in the head with the butt of an M-16 rifle.

When the realization hit me about what was going on, I scrambled to my knees, grabbed hold of the rear of the bustle rack of the turret, and hoisted myself onto the turret roof, just in time to hear the explosion of a round landing a few dozen meters away (and see SGT Planter disappear inside the turret through my loader's hatch). I fell inside the hatch, closed it up, looked at SGT Planter and mouthed "thanks." The whole troop was scrambling to back down into hide positions, while the squadron command net was blistering with reports of artillery fire and orders to displace.

In the turret, SGT Planter properly took up scanning his firing arc, watching in case the arty barrage was a precursor to a counter-attack by Iraqi forces. I spun my loader's hatch periscope toward the left rear of the turret, maintaining what air observation I could, as the LT was guiding SPC Thomas backward down the hill we were hidden behind. After a bit, we were down far enough that we couldn't see over the top of the ridgeline any more—in tank parlance, we were in a "hide" position, where none of the tank at all, not the hull, turret, or any of the TC's cupola was exposed to observation by the enemy—and the LT ordered SPC Thomas to give a hard right backward to turn around. SGT Planter kept the gun tube pointed toward the enemy, as I felt the jerking on the controls and the acceleration as Errol whipped our tank around at high speed. Oriented with the tank facing west, and the turret facing east, we high-tailed to the new assembly area and awaited additional orders. During our evac, I asked SGT Planter how long I had been sleeping, and he thought for a moment and said, "just a couple of minutes."

It felt like hours. Truly, I felt invigorated. Partly that was the epinephrine coursing through my arteries after having been rudely awakened from what was likely a near-immediate drop from wakefulness into delta sleep, and also feeling lucky I was only bad aim—or worse timing—from being permanently attached to the land in Iraq, courtesy of an Iraqi artillery round. Partly, though, even a couple of minutes of sleep seemed to rejuvenate me, and I was much more alert.

After an electric few minutes waiting for the Iraqi counter-attack to materialize over the ridgeline, the squadron command net chirped to life with a new FRAGO, and the LT started mapping our new objective. There was some back-and-forth with the various commanders, including our Troop commander, and a new destination and mission were assigned. 3d ACR, as well as 24th Infantry Division, were establishing blocking positions to prevent the Republican Guard from simply retreating back across the Euphrates River, maybe about a hundred kilometers west of Az Zubayr and just south of the marshland on the south bank of the river valley. We had accomplished all of our objectives to this point and were given some follow-on missions to support the efforts of VII Corps, to our south, in rendering the Republican Guard incapable of continued operations.

One of these missions was to move a few kilometers to the East, to set up a blocking position on the right flank of the 24th, and the left flank of VII Corps and establish a screen line—one of those missions the ACR is designed to perform. We ferried the LT to a meeting at the Troop TOC, where the updated orders were given and some additional information was disseminated. Of that, there were some "Lessons Learned" already available from the VII Corps' actions at both Medina Ridge, and the battle of 73 Easting. One of those, and the one I think that was the least surprising yet most assuring was that of all the advantages our tanks had perhaps the most glaring was our ability to use the thermal imaging system to acquire and engage enemy targets at ranges well beyond that at which the Iraqi tanks could effectively fire. This by itself was a tremendous advantage, but also had been drilled into our heads from the very beginning (not only of Desert Shield but in general). He who sees the enemy first shoots first, and shooting first equals killing first. Our tanks were, in some cases, able to acquire enemy tanks at 3000+ meters, and able to engage and destroy them on the first shot at ranges well over 2500+ meters with something like 90% first-shot hits. The sabot round of the 120 mm M1A1 was easily able to penetrate frontal turret and hull armor of the Iraqi tanks at those ranges and was achieving catastrophic kills of those targets with those long-range, first-shot hits. Additionally, we learned that several M1 tanks had taken direct hits from enemy tanks, some at very, very close range (less than 400 meters, in at least one case) and survived intact.

There had been some issues with friendly fire, and we were warned to try harder to positively identify vehicles before firing on them. The Iraqis were not without some positives; their defense against the attack of the 1st Armored at Medina Ridge was shown as an effective method for them. They had arrayed a defense using a technique called a 'reverse slope' defense, where instead of being at or in front of the ridgeline, able to look across a long expanse of terrain, they were behind it, prepared to engage units as they crested the ridgeline. It didn't help much; the 1st Armored still didn't have any tank casualties due to enemy fire, but the rest of the US Army was given the heads-up about this action as a planning tool to enable us to anticipate and react to known enemy tactics.

After retrieving the LT and resuming our role on the screen line, there were some preparations. First, we were ordered to prepare in-place for what could be described as our "anvil" role; that is, if the VII Corps advance continued, we'd be the Anvil to their Hammer: they would drive the enemy toward us, and we'd be sitting in prepared positions to destroy the enemy with long-range firepower as the VII Corps continued to push them. Engineers came and prepared hasty defensive positions, and we set up a sleep and guard plan for the second time. This time, I volunteered for first guard duty. I was assigned to a walking patrol, given a radio and night vision goggles and my Driver Errol was assigned to patrol with me while one of the other tanks put a watch in their TC's .50 cal spot. We did our patrols, were relieved at the appropriate time, and finally got a chance to sleep.

This time, we did sleep. We got several hours worth of sleep, in fact. We were roused about 04:50 or so (28 FEB) and had a few minutes to tidy up and get ourselves into our highest state of readiness and alertness. After so doing, we took a few moments to finish up some basic maintenance tasks, walking track and checking various bolts for tightness, looking at our fuel and other consumable levels (hub lubrication and shock absorbers, for example), and so forth. We had an MRE breakfast, and while we were consuming it, another FRAGO came over the squadron command net: at 07:45 local time there would commence a large-scale artillery barrage, which would continue for about 16 minutes; then, at 08:01 local time, there would be a ceasefire. We were stunned, frankly. I think we were all pretty much in disbelief about the message, and so nothing really changed for us, at that time.

Right on cue, at 07:45 local time, we could hear artillery and rocket fire commence. All of it seemed to be outbound; we never heard or saw anything coming back in our direction. At 08:01, silence.

Silence.

After about a quarter of a minute mostly spent craning our necks, as if incredulous at the lack of sounds of military activity, a great "WHOOP!" was let out by one or other of our nearby troop mates, and we gave a little prayer and celebrated: we did it! We lived, we were going to make it home.

After a few moments of celebrating, our platoon sergeant refocused us on our other tasks: continuing maintenance, making sure guard rotations were still in effect, resuming our tanker duties. After what seemed like only a few minutes, but was, in reality, probably about an hour or an hour and a half, the radio sparked to life again: another FRAGO. One of the problems with cutting off an enemy unit completely from their communications is that, in case there is a ceasefire, not all units may be aware of it, and continue to act as if the conflict is still in full effect. It's a common problem in warfare, and has happened numerous times throughout history, where a combatant unaware of the cessation of hostilities will engage an enemy, and the battle continues for a short time. Well, that's what happened to us.

Just a little bit after the ceasefire kicked in, the Iraqis shot down an aircraft not too far away from our location. A rescue mission was launched, and the medical helicopter sent to retrieve the downed pilot was also shot down. The chopper was about ten or so kilometers from our location, just to the west of Ar Rumaylah airfield. We were ordered to secure the crash site, destroy any enemy air defense in the area, and secure the airfield.

We mustered, received some additional information from the command net, and then began our assault eastward yet again. As we approached the crash site (which was to the north of my tank by a kilometer or so, in the Eagle troop 2/3 ACR sector), we started to encounter some bunker complexes and had to take up immediate RPG guard position; now, in addition to scanning the rear air for enemy aircraft, I also had to keep an eye out on the ground for RPG teams that might pop up from behind us, and take them out before they could fire on our tanks. I was eagle-eyed, maintaining a constant focus on every dip, bunker, or small rock where an enemy infantryman might try to cause my tank crew harm, but fortunately, these were all empty. As we approached the ridgeline ahead, the scout platoon radioed contact with enemy forces, dug in tanks and PCs with anti-aircraft vehicles. The troop commander ordered an "action left" drill, where we began to move into position to react to enemy forces to our left. SGT Planter was acquiring targets in his firing sector. Eagle Troop to our north was also preparing for a hasty attack.

We had clear shots at the air defense vehicles that were arrayed on the southern end of the airfield. "GUNNER HEAT AA" started the fire command from the LT.

"IDENTIFIED" replied SGT Planter.

"UP!" I yelled, signifying that the HEAT round in the main gun breech was loaded and the gun was armed.

"FIRE" ordered the LT.

"ON THE WAY!" SGT Planter's first shot at his target was prematurely detonated by an unseen fence between us and it; his second shot destroyed it utterly. "We got it!!" was SGT Planter's reply as the target exploded, and he and I exchanged a high-5 over the breech of the main gun.

I loaded a third HEAT round, yelled "UP!" into the intercom, and waited for SGT Planter to identify his next target. As I was head-down in the turret, I didn't see the actual target, but believed it to be a BMP (a Soviet-style armored infantry vehicle); according to our LT, it may have been an ammunition bunker on the airfield instead. Downrange the round went, followed by a shout of "TARGET" by SGT Planter and the clanking of the aft cap on the turret floor as I slammed another HEAT round into the main gun. "UP!" I replied as I loaded that round. Since the LT had not ordered a different kind of ammunition—and, with good reason, since all of the targets SGT Planter was engaging were targets against which HEAT is the appropriate ammo—I just kept throwing HEAT rounds into the main gun. Just for the record, HEAT is the heavier of the two types of rounds we had available, and being a Loader is exhausting when tossing HEAT rounds around, shot after shot. I was working hard, but my buddies were in danger and I had to keep my reputation as the fastest loader in the Troop, so I kept slinging them. SGT Planter then identified enemy troops in the open, and eventually engaged them with his coaxial machine gun.

After what must have been a minute or two, we were ordered to continue to advance on the airfield, secure it, and await additional orders. Partly this was because in our haste we hadn't reported our activity to higher headquarters, the Squadron commander LTC Hardy, and he was anxious for an update. The LT gave his report, and we continued moving. We complied, and as we were approaching the burnt-out hulks of vehicles just on the outskirts of the airfield defenses, the scout platoon warned of a minefield at the airfield's edge. They marked the edges of it as best they could, and we bypassed to the south of the airfield. Engineers would come in after us, and take care of that little problem, so we continued our eastward advance.

As we were bypassing the mines, another FRAGO came: we were to advance to an OBJECTIVE to our east, where an enemy position had been seen by air crews, and secure it. Scouts front in a V formation, tank platoons behind in a line, we continued attacking eastward through undulating sand and rock terrain.

T-72 in the "crater" formations we discovered

"RED 1, RED 3: CONTACT FRONT TANKS AND PCs OUT!" came from the lead scout vehicle; and Cyclone Troop began a new battle drill. The scout CFVs were using their 25 mm cannons to engage BMPs, while we were racing forward to find and destroy enemy tanks and other vehicles. The scout platoon leader reported to the Troop commander, while the Troop XO was relaying to the Squadron commander on the Squadron command net. As we approached the burning hulk of a BMP earlier destroyed by the scouts, we stopped for a moment to assess what had happened. Over the radio, we heard the Platoon Sergeant excitedly reporting T-72s nearby, and the LT and I popped out of our hatches and realized that we were hip-deep into an enemy encampment. The unit was a headquarters element of a Brigade of one of the Republican Guard divisions, and there were T-72s, BRDMs (another Soviet-style armored infantry vehicle), trucks, jeeps, and portable trailers in what looked like simple craters dug out of the ground; from ground level more than a few meters away, they were invisible. I was later told that this complex was a mine quarry, which the Iraqi forces had apparently turned into a ready-made hide position.

The LT reported to the Troop Commander that we'd stumbled into an enemy encampment, and needed to clear it before moving forward. While waiting for the scouts to return, we were attacked by what appeared to be a single rifleman with his AK-47; I engaged and dropped him with my loader's M240 machine gun.

The next few hours was spent guarding this location, as the intel guys came through. It turned out to be a pretty high-level headquarters for the Republican Guard unit and included the capture of a Brigade commander-equivalent CO of the Iraqi army, and a trailer full of encryption equipment, plans, maps, and such.

After the site was cleared we were ordered to occupy positions a few kilometers East. We halted and established defensive positions overlooking a local road system (which, as it turns out, was Highway 8 and Freeway 1).

Once our defensive positions were established, the Troop immediately setup a LOGPAC (resupply) and we took tanks back into a hide position one at a time to perform immediate maintenance. Due to the engine of the tank being a turbine, and ingesting tremendous amounts of air, there are very large air filters that protect the engine from dust. Among a few other things, this requires the air filters be cleaned out whenever possible, and so each tank had to back down, shut down its engine, and then position the turret just so. Once positioned, the hatches covering the filters could be opened and the filters themselves removed. Under ideal circumstances, we would have a high-pressure air hose available to blow the contaminants out, but this was hardly an ideal circumstance. We took the filters out and gently banged them against the side of the hull or the top of the back deck until the dust fell out. Then, we'd put them back and fire up the engine, sweep off the dust, and walk the track on the way back to our defensive position. If we found any loose or missing center guides or wedge bolts on the track, we'd immediately fix or replace them. Then as soon as we were back in position, we'd top off track tension and start cleaning weapons, one at a time.

When the supply trucks showed up (the Heavy Expanded Mobility Tactical Truck, or HEMTT, that brought fuel & other petroleum products, ammo, or food & other supplies) we restocked main gun and machine gun ammo, topped off the fuel, and grabbed whatever other supplies we could. Then, off the truck would go to the next tank in the line.

Captured Iraqi artillery piece (just left of and behind "^ C6"), which we later used as a gunnery practice target

From our commanding defensive position overlooking those highways we stayed in this position for several more days. During that time, the 24th Infantry Division to our north reporting being fired upon from the highway, and engaged enemy units there; we were ordered to stay in a position to counter-attack if the 24th got into a protracted fight but never did get involved in that particular action.

Over the next several days, we performed our normal maintenance duties, did guard patrols, did some gunnery practice, and finally got a chance to eat some hot food. Mail arrived, some of it more than a week old already. We relished the opportunity to reconnect our brains with the thoughts of our loved ones and being able to actually see them again, someday. It didn't take long; our heavy equipment was secured and transported in mid-March, and we flew out of the sandbox late on the 16 March, 1991.

At first, the flight was energizing and exciting, as we all really—finally—felt safe. Safer than we'd felt in months, to be sure. After lifting off from Saudi Arabia and reaching our cruising altitude, the crew showed us the video of *Voices that Care*, the song written by Linda Thompson, David Foster, and Peter Cetera for the service members in the Gulf. We had no idea this song or video existed; it was a welcome sight to see how much support there had been in the US for our efforts, and most of us were moved—some, including me myself, to silent tears—at seeing the video. Other videos of various kinds were shown, and most of us either went to sleep or stayed up talking about our experiences. Along with our unit, there was a TV camera crew from a Minnesota TV station on the plane. They filmed our journey home and did several individual interviews mostly with soldiers from the area near the TV station's audience. We landed in Germany and deplaned into the same USO area where we'd originally been in on the way into the sandbox in the first place. The paper graffiti was much more elaborate than when we'd originally visited, of course, and several of us immediately took to the phone bank to make quick collect phone calls to family members. I reached my family in Tucson to at least let them know I was safe, and on our way back to the US.

After a couple of hours to refuel the aircraft and change crews, we took off again. This time, we were bound for the grandness of La Guardia airport in New York City. It was nighttime when we took off, so almost all of us ended up sleeping for most of the flight over the Atlantic. As we approached US airspace, with the sun rising and most of us awake and preparing to deplane for a short time, the TV crew started filming again. The pilot came over the intercom, and announced that we were officially in US airspace, and the entire cabin erupted in screams, shouts, and the woofing of elated tankers and cav scouts. A few minutes later, our Squadron commander came over the intercom, and announced that because of the layover we would have in the airport, we were each permitted to have TWO regular sized beers in the airport, and that was all. No spirits, no wine, and no more than two beers. One of our troopers was from New York City or the surrounding area, and when we deplaned his wife was there to greet him; knowing in advance this was true he had been granted an immediate leave and would report back to Ft. Bliss a few days later.

The rest of us were greeted by a small but vocal group of supporters, who hugged and high-fived us as we came out of the jetway and into the terminal. Most of us then immediately set out to locate an open watering hole, only to be quite dismayed to find out that none of them were open! As we milled about, apparently one of the vendors got wind that a plane full of soldiers from the Gulf War were in the terminal and eager to buy beer, and he made a special trip to open his small beer concessionary. We were in business—as it were—and many of us took advantage of our CO's permission to consume the two beers we were allotted.

After the plane was yet again refueled and the crew switched out, we re-boarded and took off for El Paso International Airport, arriving in El Paso in the early afternoon of 18 March, 1991. We were greeted on the tarmac by one of the Army Bands (I believe the 62nd Army band), playing traditional Army marching music, and just before we disembarked we were treated to a short but epic speech from our Squadron commander, which went in part: "Brave Rifles! Veterans! You are heroes not only in the eyes of the Army but also in the eyes of your Nation, and it is your Nation that stands ready to greet you." Finally, we were permitted to deplane, and meet the throng of family and friends who were assembled there. We turned in our personal weapons and after a short briefing and prayer, we were released to our friends and families. My parents had come out from Tucson, and we went to their motel room to drop off a few personal belongings and then went to dinner—a family again, reunited after the apprehension and uncertainty of war.

I believe we delivered the message of the United Nations, and that emphatically: if you don't leave Kuwait, we will destroy your military. There are questions about the long-term effect of Desert Storm, and some who believe that we didn't go far enough—that we should have turned left, and headed straight to Baghdad—but I'm satisfied with the mission we executed. Our unit, in particular, was quite fortunate. We had no soldiers killed in action. We had no soldiers seriously wounded in action. We performed every mission we were given, and even though not everything that we did was letter-perfect, it was done with the utmost of professionalism and in the greatest tradition of the Brave Rifles and the US Army.

Some of 2nd Platoon, C Troop, 1/3 ACR displaying a captured Iraqi Tanker's helmet after our attack through the Republican Guard.

The author, posing with the same helmet as in the previous picture.

Other Books by Bacil Donovan Warren

Hooray for Pain!: Poetry and Prose about embracing life's difficulty in order to overcome it. Available at many stores online.

Universo Responsoriis (Fermi's Paradox answered: a novel). Coming soon.

About the Author

An Army veteran of Desert Shield and Desert Storm, as well as a former Paramedic and an IT professional, Bacil Donovan Warren writes poetry, veteran-focused non-fiction, and sci-fi, and blogs about writing and technology.

Connect with Bacil Donovan Warren:

Web: http://www.bacildonovanwarren.com/
Facebook: http://www.facebook.com/BacilDonovanWarren
Twitter: http://www.twitter.com/BacilDonovan
Email: bdw@bacildonovanwarren.com
Blog:
   Cogitations of a Semi-Pro Wordsmith http://blog.bacildonovanwarren.com/

Made in the USA
Lexington, KY
17 December 2018